Dedication

In a year unlike any other, we dedicate this
book to the brilliantly resilient children of
Whitnash Primary School.

CONTENTS

SAVOURY
DISHES

CHEESEBURGER PASTA

Contributed by: Mckenzie - Year 4

INGREDIENTS:

455g (1lb) of extra lean ground beef
1 onion, finely chopped
2 medium fresh tomatoes, peeled and chopped
2 tbs of tomato paste
1 tsp of paprika
1/2 tsp of onion powder
1/2 tsp of garlic powder
1/2 tsp of mustard powder
Pinch of salt and black pepper
1/2 tbs of Worcestershire sauce
1 tbs of sukrin gold (or another sweetener of choice)
300g (10.5oz) of uncooked penne pasta (or other pasta of choice)
4 cups (960ml) of chicken stock
2-3 tbs of chopped pickles.
120g (4oz) of cheddar cheese - reserve a little for sprinkling on top once cooked
Fresh chopped Italian parsley
Spray Oil

This is Mckenzie's favourite dish at home and he loves to get involved in the cooking.

METHOD:

1. Add to a small bowl the paprika, garlic powder, onion powder, mustard powder, salt and black pepper and mix to combine.

2. Spray a frying pan with spray oil and over a medium-high heat add the ground beef and onion and cook until brown.

3. Add the spices, tomatoes, tomato paste, Worcestershire sauce and sukrin and mix to coat.

4. Stir in the penne pasta.

5. Add the stock, bring to a boil, cover and simmer for 10-12 mins

6. Remove lid, add chopped pickles and cheese and stir until sauce is velvety and coats everything in the pan.

7. Sprinkle with fresh chopped Italian parsley and the reserved cheese.

8. Enjoy with a side salad.

MRS FORD'S 'THROW IT TOGETHER' WRAPS

Contributed by: Mrs Ford

Marinade time: 1 hour
Preheat oven if serving fries/wedges

INGREDIENTS:

One Tortilla wrap per person
1 chicken breast portion per person
50g diced bacon
1-2 tbsp Dark Soy Sauce per chicken breast
Optional extras
Grated Cheddar cheese (about 30g per person)
Salad of your choice
Sauce/dressing of your choice
Fries or potato wedges

METHOD:

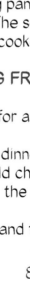

1. Chop chicken & bacon into chunks and place in separate dishes.

2. Cover the chicken in soy sauce ~ pop in the fridge for 1 hour to marinade.

3. While the chicken marinades, grate some cheese & prepare some salad in fine slices. Place these in the fridge.

4. Heat oil in a large frying pan and add the chicken and brown for about 10 minutes on a high heat ~ The soy sauce should turn a golden colour and the chicken chunks should be cooked through.

   IF YOU ARE SERVING FRIES, ADD THESE TO THE OVEN NOW

5. Add the bacon and fry for another 10-20 minutes

6. Lay out wraps on large dinner plates and spoon the cooked chicken and bacon onto each wrap. Add cheese, salad and sauces to each diner's liking and fold the tortillas. (Use the tortilla packet for how to fold).

7. Serve with extra salad and fries ~ Tuck in and enjoy!

BUTTERNUT MACARONI CHEESE WITH BACON

Contributed by: Kyle - Year 2

Serves: 4

INGREDIENTS:

3 bacon medallions all fat removed chopped into pieces.
1 diced onion
Macaroni pasta made up to packet instructions
1 tsp of garlic granules
1 bag of frozen butternut squash chunks
Chicken stock
160g low fat cheddar
Parsley (optional)
Salt and pepper to taste

Kyle's favourite dish! He particularly likes watching mum blend the sauce and eating it!

METHOD:

1. Make up pasta to packet instructions.

2. Whilst that's cooking, fry the bacon and onion and garlic powder in a pan with spray oil or 1/2 tbsp of good quality oil.

3. In another pan put the whole bag of the butternut squash chunks and top with chicken stock until just about covered.

4. Once cooked, blitz the butternut squash with a hand blender until smooth, it should look like a really thick soup. Add the cheese and blitz again.

5. Add the pasta and bacon mix and stir thoroughly.

6. Either serve immediately or pop into an oven proof dish and grill the top for a little extra flavour. Sprinkle on your parsley.

7. Serve with salad or vegetables of you're choice.

SATURDAY PASTA

Contributed by: Bayleaf Cookery School

Preparation time: 20-25 minutes
Serves: 4

INGREDIENTS:

Olive oil
1 medium/ large red onion, chopped
A reasonable pinch of dried chilli seeds (size of the pinch to vary according to taste)
1/2 - 1 teaspoon cinnamon
Medium bunch of fresh basil leaves, separated from stalks (stalks finely chopped)
1 tin chopped tomatoes
2x tins tuna in oil
Salt & pepper
500g bag of Rigatoni pasta
Zest of a lemon
Juice of 1/2 a lemon
Handful of grated parmesan cheese (ideally fresh)

bayleaf
cookery school

@bayleafcookeryschool

Bayleafcookeryschool.co.uk

METHOD:

1. Heat a slug of olive oil in a medium sized heavy bottomed pan on a low-medium heat and add basil stalks, cinnamon and onion. Fry until onion soft and turning translucent - about 8-10 mins - stirring fairly continuously to ensure the mixture doesn't burn.

2. Add tomatoes and tuna, season to taste and stir well, turning up heat slightly and bringing to a simmer.

3. At around the same time as you add the tuna and tomato, put the pasta on to cook, adding the Rigatoni to a large pan of lightly salted boiling water. Cook until the pasta has just a little bit of bite then drain and return to the pan with a little olive oil to stop it sticking.

4. Roughly tear the basil leaves and add them to the sauce along with the lemon zest and juice and the grated parmesan. Add to the pasta and mix well.

5. Serve in bowls.

CHICKEN BUNNY CHOW

Contributed by: Mrs Theunissen

Preparation time: 30 minutes
Cooking time: 1 hour
Serves: 4

As Mrs Theunissen is from South Africa, she thought you would like a South African dish!

INGREDIENTS:

1 star anise
1 cinnamon stick
3 whole cardamom pods
1 tbsp vegetable oil
1 onion, chopped
10 fresh curry leaves
1 garlic clove, finely chopped
2 1/2 tbsp garam masala
1 tsp cayenne pepper
2 tsp turmeric
2 beef tomatoes, chopped
1kg pack chicken drumsticks and thighs, skin removed

1 baking potato, peeled and cubed
1 tbsp cornflour
15g (1/2oz) chopped fresh coriander leaves, reserving a few whole leaves to garnish
2 tbsp lime juice
2 small farmhouse loaves, halved and hollowed
Cook's tip: Tear the hollowed-out bread into breadcrumbs and freeze for stuffings and crunchy coatings.

METHOD:

1. In a dry frying pan over a low-medium heat, place the star anise, cinnamon stick and cardamom pods and heat for 2-3 minutes until fragrant, shaking the pan occasionally and turning the spices.

2. Add the oil and onion and fry over a medium heat, stirring occasionally, for 5 minutes. Add the curry leaves and garlic and fry for a further 5 minutes, stirring occasionally.

3. Stir in the garam masala, cayenne pepper and turmeric and fry for a further minute, then add the tomatoes and cook for a further minute. Add the chicken drumsticks and thighs and turn to coat in the spiced tomato and onion mixture. Pour in 500ml cold water and bring to the boil then reduce the heat, cover and simmer for 30 minutes, stirring occasionally.

4. Add the potato and simmer, uncovered, for a further 15 minutes until the potatoes are tender. Remove from the heat. Remove the chicken pieces using a slotted spoon. Use two forks to shred the meat to remove it from the bones. Set the meat aside and discard the bones and any skin.

5. Mix the cornflour with 2 tbsp cold water then stir the cornflour paste through the curry sauce, bring to the boil, stirring continuously, until thickened. Remove the star anise and cinnamon stick, then return the chicken to the pan and mix well. Stir through the chopped coriander and lime juice. Spoon into the hollowed-out loaves and garnish with the reserved coriander leaves.

CHICKPEA, SPINACH & POTATO CURRY

Contributed by: Mrs Lane

Preparation time: 30 minutes
Cooking time: 1 hour
Serves: 4

INGREDIENTS:

3 large potatoes
1 large sweet potato
2 tbsp sunflower or groundnut oil
1 large or 2 medium onions, finely chopped
4 garlic cloves, crushed
2 tbsp korma curry past
400g can chickpeas
500ml water or vegetable stock
Juice of 1 lemon
200ml carton coconut cream
1 tbsp mango chutney
1 tbsp tomato puree
4 tbsps. Chopped fresh coriander leaves
200g can chopped tomatoes
2 tbsps. Ground almonds (optional)
Big handful of spinach leaves
Salt

If you want to make the RAITA
Finely chop a 10cm piece of cucumber. Mix with 1 chopped spring onion, 2 crushed garlic cloves, 6 tbsp natural yogurt and seasoning.

METHOD:

1. Peel both types of potato and cut into bite-size chunks.

2. Heat oil in a large heavy bottomed saucepan. Add the onions, garlic and a pinch of salt and cook until transparent.

3. Stir in the curry paste. Cook for 2 minutes. Add the potatoes and chickpeas. Stir until coated. Cook for 1 minute.

4. Add water or stock, lemon juice, coconut cream, mango chutney, tomato puree, two thirds of the coriander, tomatoes and almonds (if using). Turn up the heat to boil, stirring occasionally.

5. Reduce heat, cover and simmer very gently for 45 minutes, at least. Stir in spinach and cook for 2-3 minutes, until wilted.

6. Taste and adjust by adding more curry paste, lemon juice or tomato puree to taste. Throw rest of coriander on top. Eat with rice, nan, cucumber raita, poppadoms and chutney.

YUK SUNG

Contributed by: Mrs Stevenson

Cooking time: 1 hour
Serves: 4

INGREDIENTS:

1 tbsp olive oil
1 onion
3 cloves garlic
1 tsp ginger puree or 1 inch piece if using fresh.
2 small carrots
250g mushrooms
500g pork mince
3 tsp Chinese five spice
2 tbsp dark soy sauce
2 tbsp oyster sauce
2 tbsp light soy sauce
To Serve
3 spring onions, chopped
2 red chillies (add more or less depending on your taste)
2-3 little gem lettuce

METHOD:

1. Firstly prepare your vegetables:
     a. Chop onion and mushrooms.
     b. Peel and crush garlic.
     c. Peel and finely chop carrots.
     d. Peel and chop ginger (if using fresh).
2. Heat half the oil in large open wok, fry the pork mince until browned. Then remove from pan and stand to the side.
3. Add the rest of the oil to the pan and fry onion, garlic and ginger for around 3 minutes until soft.
4. Add mushrooms and carrots, fry for a further 5 minutes.
5. Put pork back in the frying pan, add in five spice, dark and light soy and oyster sauces.
6. Cook on a medium to low heat for 10-15 minutes, until the mixture is browned, sauce has thicken slightly and absorbed into the meat.
7. Serve in little gem lettuce leaves, and top with chopped spring onions and chillies. (Leave chillies out if you prefer).

DESSERTS

NO BAKE MINI EGG CHEESECAKE

Contributed by: Mrs Bowyer

Preparation time: 15 minutes
Serves: 12

INGREDIENTS:

280g Digestive Chocolate Biscuits
140g Unsalted Butter (melted)
360g Mini eggs, plus 270g to decorate (about 7 small bags in total)
550ml Double cream, plus 50ml to decorate (lightly whipped until it forms soft peaks)
140g icing sugar sifted
2 x 280g tubs of full fat cream cheese
Juice of half a lemon

METHOD:

1. Crush the biscuits until they look like lumpy sand (you can do this in a food processor).

2. Mix with the melted butter and press into a 7" tin

3. Chop 360g of the mini eggs in half.

4. Combine the whipped cream, icing sugar, cream cheese, lemon juice and chopped mini eggs. Fold in gently until fully combined.

5. Smooth on top of the biscuit base and flatten the top with the back of a spoon or a palette knife.

6. Chill for two hours or over night.

7. Remove the cheesecake from the tin.

8. Put the remaining whipped cream on top of the cheesecake and put on the remaining mini eggs (some chopped in half).

9. Share and enjoy.

CAKES & BREAD

LIMONCELLO CAKE

Contributed by Mrs Ellison

Preheat oven 175°C / gas mark 4
Prepare sandwich tins: 3 x 15cm (6") round

INGREDIENTS:

For the Sponge
200g unsalted butter, softened
200g caster sugar
Pinch of salt
Finely grated zest of 2 unwaxed lemons
4 medium eggs
200g self-raising flour

For the sugar syrup
150ml caster sugar
50ml of Limoncello Liqueur

For the buttercream filling
80g unsalted butter
80g icing sugar, sifted
Pinch of salt
40g of good quality lemon jelly or lemon curd

METHOD:

To make the sponge
1. Place the butter, sugar, salt and lemon zest into a mixing bowl and cream together until pale and fluffy.
2. Beat the eggs lightly in another bowl and slowly add to the butter mixture while whisking quickly. If the mixture starts to separate or curdle, stop adding the egg and beat in 2-3 tablespoons of flour. This will rebind the batter. Once all the egg has been added and combined with the butter mixture, sift in the flour and stir until the batter is just combined. This will ensure the sponges stay light and fluffy.
3. Divide the batter evenly between the sandwich tins. If you find it difficult to measure by eye, use your kitchen scales to weigh out the amount of sponge mixture in each tin.
4. Bake for 15-20 minutes, depending on your oven. If you are using deeper cake tins, the sponges will take longer to cook. The sponges are cooked when the sides are beginning to shrink away from the edge of the tins and the tops are golden brown and spring back to the touch. If in doubt, insert a clean knife or skewer into the center of each sponge; it should come out clean.

Continued ...

LIMONCELLO CAKE Continued ...

To make the sugar syrup

1. While the sponges are baking, prepare the sugar syrup for soaking. Place the lemon juice and caster sugar in a saucepan and bring to the boil. Simmer until all the sugar crystals have dissolved. Set aside to cool down slightly and then add the Limoncello liqueur.
2. Once the sponges are baked, let them rest for about 10 minutes outside the oven. Using a pastry brush, soak the tops of the sponges with the syrup while they are still warm; this allows the syrup to be absorbed faster.
3. Once just warm, run a knife all the way round the sides of the tins, remove the sponges from the tins and leave to cool completely on a wire rack.
4. Once cool, wrap the sponges in cling film and then rest them over night at room temperature. This will ensure that all the moisture is sealed in and the sponges firm up to the perfect texture for trimming and layering.

To make the buttercream filling

Place the butter, icing sugar and salt into a mixing bowl and cream together until pale and fluffy. Add the lemon jelly to the mixture and stir through until combined and smooth.

To assemble the cake

1. Trim and sandwich together the three sponge layers using one-third of the buttercream filling and the limoncello syrup for soaking. With the remaining buttercream filling, cover the top of the cake. Alternatively, there should be enough to mask the top and sides of the cake, using a turn-table.
2. Chill until set. Add some decorations of choice.
3. Serve the cake at room temperature.

This cake is best enjoyed within 3 days of baking, but it can last up to 1 week.

VE DAY RATION BOOK TEACAKE

Contributed by: Olivia - Year 2

Preheat oven 180°C
Cooking time: 30-35 minutes

INGREDIENTS:

567 ml tea (made with boiling water and teabag, then teabag removed)
170g butter
170g sugar
170g sultanas
280g self-raising flour
2 tsp mixed spice

METHOD:

1. Place the butter, sugar, sultanas and tea in a pan.

2. Heat over a hob until all the butter has melted. Leave to cool.

3. In a bowl place the flour and mixed spice.

4. When cool, pour the liquid mixture into the dry mixture in the bowl. Mix thoroughly to combine.

5. Pour the mixture into a prepared 8" cake tin.

6. Bake in a preheated oven for 30-35 minutes or until a knife comes out clean.

BLACKBERRY BAKEWELLS

Contributed by: Bayleaf Cooker School

Preheat oven 200°C/180°C fan/gas mark 6
Cooking time: 20 minutes

INGREDIENTS:

For the pastry
225g plain flour
100g unsalted butter, straight from the fridge, chopped into cubes
Pinch salt
2-3 tbsp cold water

For the filling
1 tbsp plain flour
100g unsalted butter
100g caster sugar
1 egg, beaten
100g ground almonds
150g blackberries
25g flaked almonds

 @bayleafcookeryschool

 Bayleafcookeryschool.co.uk

METHOD:

Pastry
Sieve the flour into a bowl and add a pinch of salt.
Add cubed butter and rub between thumbs and fingers until no lumps of butter remain and the mixture resembles breadcrumbs.
Add one tbsp of cold water, mixing it in with your hand, then more water as required until you can bring the pastry mixture together into a smooth but non-sticky ball.
Ideally you should let the pastry sit in the fridge for a minimum of half an hour before rolling it out but if you don't have time, leave this stage out. If you do have time to refrigerate, don't forget to take the pastry out of in time to let it warm up again before rolling as it's hard to roll when cold.
Roll out the pastry on a floured surface and cut out 12 circles with a cutter.
Line the holes of a muffin tin with the pastry circles and set aside.

Filling
Beat together the butter, caster sugar, egg, ground almonds and flour.
Spoon mixture into each pastry circles.
Press 2-3 blackberries into the filling of each individual Bakewell, then scatter flaked almonds over the top.
Bake for approximately 20 minutes until lightly golden. Leave to cool slightly before removing them from the tin.
These can be eaten warm or cold and will freeze well.
Serve with a dollop of clotted cream.

EASY APPLE CAKE

Contributed by: Mrs Ellison

Preheat oven: 180°C/Fan 160°C/Gas 4
Cooking time: 1¼ hours

INGREDIENTS:

250g cooking apples (peeled weight)
175g self-raising flour
175g caster sugar, plus extra to sprinkle
2 large eggs
½ tsp almond extract
100g butter, melted

METHOD:

1. Preheat the oven as above and line a 20cm loose-bottomed cake or springform tin with non-stick baking paper.

It is best to use a loose-bottomed cake or springform tin for this as it is often difficult to turn out. If you do not have one, line the base of an ordinary tin with foil or baking paper and, after allowing it to cool, carefully turn out on to a flat plate. Then peel off the foil or paper and reverse the cake onto another plate.

2. Thinly slice the apples and put them in a bowl of water.

3. Measure the flour into a bowl with the sugar. Beat the eggs and almond extract together and stir them into the flour, together with the melted butter, and mix well. Spread half this mixture into the tin.

4. Drain and dry the apples on kitchen paper and arrange them on the cake mixture. Top with the remaining cake mixture; it is not very easy to spread but if the apples show through it doesn't matter too much.

5. Bake in the preheated oven for 1¼ hours, or until golden and shrinking slightly from the sides of the tin.

6. Leave to cool for 15 minutes then turn out and remove the paper.

7. Sift over some caster sugar and serve warm with cream.

KIERA'S SCONE RECIPE

Contributed by: Kiera

Preheat oven: 220°c, 200°c fan, gas mark 6
Cooking time: 15 minutes

INGREDIENTS:

50g unsalted butter
200g self-raising white flour
1 tbsp. white caster sugar
1 pinch salt
125 ml milk

Kiera's Top Tip No: 1
Try not to over mix or handle/roll the dough too much. Your scones won't rise as much

Kiera's Top Tip No: 2
Slice shallow cuts into the top of the dough to make your scones grow bigger.

METHOD:

1. Preheat the oven as above.

2. Line a baking sheet with parchment.

3. Rub the butter into the flour, until the mixture resembles breadcrumbs. Stir in the sugar and salt.

4. Make a well in the middle of the mixture and stir in the milk until even and the dough come together.

5. Put the dough onto a floured surface and shape into a thick square. Don't handle the dough too much.

6. Use a cookie cutter to cut your scones into your desired shape and place them onto a baking sheet.

7. Brush the top of the scones with a little milk.

8. Bake in a the preheated oven for 15 minutes until they are golden brown.

SCONES

Contributed by: Ben Stevenson

Preheat oven: 200°C
Cooking time: 10 minutes

INGREDIENTS:

8oz self-raising flour
2oz butter
1oz caster sugar
1-2oz fruit
¾ mug of milk

METHOD:

1. Preheat oven as above.

2. Measure the self-raising flour into a large bowl.

3. Measure the butter and put it in with the flour.

4. Using your finger tips, rub the flour and the butter to a breadcrumb consistency.

5. Measure the caster sugar and add it to the butter and flour mixture.

6. Measure the fruit and add it to the butter, flour and sugar mixture.

7. Heat the milk until it is luke warm.

8. Add the milk little by little to the mixture until it all comes together but is not too sticky. (You may not need it all).

9. Put it is the oven for 10 minutes and then take them out to cool.

CRUMBLE

Contributed by: Joe Stevenson

Preheat oven: 180°C
Cooking time: 30 minutes

INGREDIENTS:

8oz self-raising flour
4oz butter
2oz caster sugar, plus some to sprinkle
14oz frozen fruit
4 apples

METHOD:

1. Preheat the oven as above.

2. Weigh the flour into a bowl.

3. Weigh the butter and add to the flour

4. Mix together using the tips of your fingers until the mixture resembles breadcrumbs.

5. Weigh the caster sugar and add to the mixture.

6. Mix all ingredients together for about two minutes.

7. Peel and core the apples and cut into slices approx. 1cm wide.

8. Defrost the fruit in the microwave for two minutes.

9. Drain the fruit and add the apples.

10. Put the fruit into a 7cm deep and 21 wide bowl.

11. Put the flour mixture on top of the fruit.

12. Put into the oven and cook for 30 minutes.

RAINBOW CAKE

Contributed by: Miss Hall

Preparation time: 1 hour
Preheat oven: 170°C / Gas 3
Cooking time: 30 minutes

INGREDIENTS:

700g butter, room temperature
700g caster sugar
1½ tsp vanilla extract
9 eggs
700g self-raising flour
Food colouring: red, orange, yellow, green, blue and purple
Buttercream
400g butter, room temperature
800g icing sugar
120ml milk

If you want each layer to have a different flavour, then you can add the flavouring at the same time as the food colouring Step 2

METHOD:

Preheat oven as above and grease six 20cm cake tins and line with grease-proof paper.

For the cake

1. Beat together the butter, sugar and vanilla flavouring until pale and creamy. Add the eggs one at a time, beating well after each addition then gradually add the flour, mixing well until smooth.

2. Divide the cake mixture equally between six mixing bowls and add one food colour into each bowl and stir well, using a different spoon for each colour. Start with a small amount and then add more if needed to get the desire colour. If using a different flavour for each cake, add now.

3. Place the mixtures into the six prepared cake tins and level the top.

4. Bake the cakes for 20 minutes, or until a skewer inserted in the center comes out clean. Let the cakes cool completely.

5. Once the cakes are cool, use a sharp serrated knife to cut the tops off the cakes so that each layer is of the same height.

Continued ...

RAINBOW CAKE Continued ...

For the buttercream

1. Beat the butter until light and fluffy. Add the icing sugar gradually, mixing well. Finally mix in the milk.

2. Spread a bit of buttercream on the bottom of a serving platter or cake stand.

3. Place the purple sponge first and spread the top of the sponge with buttercream. Top with the blue sponge and repeat. Continue in this order: green, yellow, orange then red.

4. Spread the entire cake, top and sides with a thin layer of buttercream.

Decorate as desired.

BANANA BREAD

Contributed by: Miss Brown

Prparation time: 10 minutes
Cooking time: 35-40 minutes
Serves: 12

INGREDIENTS:

1 large egg
130g self-raising flour
1 tsp baking powder
55g butter, softened, plus extra for greasing
100g caster sugar
3 or 4 ripe bananas

METHOD:

1. Preheat oven 180°C/160°C fan.

2. Grease a 22cm x 12 cm loaf tin.

3. In a large bowl, mix all ingredients together, combining well with a fork. You may need to add a drop of milk to achieve a loose dropping consistency.

4. Pour into the prepared loaf tin and bake for 35-40 minutes

Very Easy!
All you need is a bowl and a fork!

BREAD

Contributed by: Mrs Bowyer

Pre-heat oven to 190°C
Preparation time: 2 ½ hours
Cooking time: 20-25 mins

INGREDIENTS:

150g Strong flour
½ tsp yeast
½ tsp sugar
¼ tsp salt
1 tbsp oil
75ml warm water

METHOD:

1. Place a zip close bag on the scales.
2. Put the dry ingredients in the bag and shake bag.
3. Add oil and water and close bag.
4. Knead all ingredients in bag for 10 to 15 minutes until the ingredients form a dough.
5. Open bag and place dough, within the bag, in a foil tray.
6. Seal bag tightly and leave to prove for about 2 hours.
7. Remove dough and tray from the bag.
8. Place the dough in the tray in a pre-heated oven (190°C).
9. Bake for 20 – 25 minutes..
10. Remove from oven, allow to cool. ENJOY!

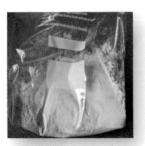

BISCUITS & PASTRIES

CHOCOLATE CHIP COOKIES

Contributed by: Mrs Bowyer

Preparation Time: 30 mins to 1 hour
Cooking Time: 10 to 30 mins
Serves: makes 18 very large cookies

INGREDIENTS

275g unsalted butter, softened
275g soft light brown sugar
225g granulated sugar
2 large eggs
1 tbsp vanilla extract
475g plain flour
2 tsp baking powder
300g milk chocolate, chopped roughly into chunks
Sea salt

METHOD

1. Preheat the oven to 180°c/350F/Gas4
2. Put the butter and sugars into a large mixing bowl. Beat together with a electric hand whisk until smooth and light in colour.
3. Add the eggs, one at a time, mixing between each one. Once the eggs are combined, add the vanilla extract.
4. Sift in the flour and baking powder and mix with a wooden spoon until completely incorporated. Add the chocolate chunks and mix in until thoroughly combined. Divide the dough in half.
5. Place each half onto a large sheet of cling film. Roll the dough into a wide sausage shape and wrap in the cling film, twisting the ends to seal. Each sausage will make nine large cookies (but you can roll them smaller and make more). The dough sausages can be frozen at this point. However if you wish to bake them straightaway, chill the dough in the fridge for 30 minutes before use.
6. Once ready to use the cookie dough, remove from the freezer and allow to warm up enough to slice.
7. Slice the dough sausage into nine discs and place onto a non-stick baking tray or a tray that has been lined with baking parchment.
8. Sprinkle each cooking with a tiny pinch of salt and bake in the preheated oven for 20 minutes, or until they are golden brown on the edge and slightly paler in the center.
9. Remove from the oven and transfer to a wire rack to cool before serving.

CINNAMON WHIRLS

Contributed by: Daro - Year 4 and Maily - Year 1

Preheat oven to 180°C

INGREDIENTS

Puff pastry
Brown sugar
Cinnamon
Cardamom
Butter

METHOD

1. Roll the puff pastry with a rolling pin so it is nice and flat.

2. Melt the butter and use a brush to spread it all over the pastry.

3. Mix the sugar, cinnamon and cardamom together and spread it all over the pastry.

4. Roll the pastry into a sausage.

5. Cut them into equal slices and leave to rest for about 10 minutes.

6. Bake in a preheated oven for 20 minutes.

NUTELLA TWISTS & WHEELS

Contributed by: Mrs Norris

Preheat oven to 200°C (fan)
Cooking time: 15-20 minutes

INGREDIENTS

Puff pastry
Nutella

METHOD

1. Gather all of your ingredients. Open out your puff pastry and allow it to reach room temperature.

2. Spread Nutella on half of the pastry.

3. Fold the top half of the pastry onto the bottom half, making a Nutella sandwich!

4. Cut half of the pastry into strips about a centimeter wide.

5. Line a baking tray with grease proof paper.

6. Hold the top of the strip of pastry and twist the bottom to make a twist and place these on the lined baking tray.

7. Continue to cut centimeter strips with the rest of the pastry.

8. To make a swirl, roll the strip to make a snail shell shape, or roll both sides into the middle.

9. Place them all on the baking tray and place in the middle of the oven for 15-20 minutes or until golden brown.

10. Remove from the oven and allow to cool.

Enjoy with a cup of tea!

CHOCOLATE CHIP COOKIES

Contributed by: Arun - Year 4

Cooking Time: 8 to 10 mins
Preheat oven to 180°C

INGREDIENTS

100g light brown sugar
125g sugar
125g butter
1 egg
225g self-raising flour
1 tsp vanilla essence
200g chocolate chips

METHOD

1. Cream the butter, sugar together

2. Add egg, then flour, then chocolate chips.

3. Roll into walnut size balls and put onto baking trays.

4. Bake in a preheated oven for 8-10 minutes until slightly golden

5. Enjoy!

CHOCOLATE CHIP COOKIES

Contributed by: Miss Brown
Chilling Time: 1 hour
Cooking Time: 10 minutes
Preheat over to 190°C/170°C fan/gas 5.

INGREDIENTS

60g cocoa powder, sieved
200g caster sugar
60ml vegetable oil
2 large eggs
180g plain flour
1tsp baking powder
70g icing sugar
Pinch of salt

These will keep for four days in a biscuit tin - if they last that long"

METHOD

1. Mix the cocoa, caster sugar and oil together. Add the eggs one at a time, whisking until fully combined.

2. Stir the flour, baking powder and salt together in a separate bowl, then add to the cocoa mixture.

3. Transfer to the fridge and chill for 1 hour.

4. Tip the icing sugar into a shallow dish

5. Form a heaped teaspoon of the dough into a ball, then roll in the sugar to coat. Repeat with the remaining dough.

6. Put dough balls evenly spaced on a baking tray lined with baking parchment.

7. Bake in the center of a pre-heated oven for 10 minutes.

8. Transfer to a wire rack and leave to cool.

PEANUT BUTTER COOKIES

Contributed by: Evelyn

Chilling Time: 1 hour
Cooking Time: 10 minutes
Preheat over to 190°C/170°C fan/gas

INGREDIENTS

200g-peanut butter
175g-caster sugar
1 egg
¼ of a tsp of salt
White chocolate chunks

Enjoy with a cup of tea!

METHOD

1. Put the ingredients into the bowl.

2. Mix them together with a wooden spoon.

3. Shape into balls.

4. Put onto baking trays.

5. Put into a preheated oven for 12 minutes

UNICORN SHORTBREAD

Contributed by: Daisy - Reception

Chilling Time: 1 hour
Cooking Time: 10 minutes
Preheat over to 190°C/170°C fan/375°F/gas 5.

INGREDIENTS

125g/4oz butter
55g/2oz caster sugar
180g/6oz plain flour
Packet of white chocolate buttons
Rainbow sprinkles or similar to decorate

You will need a Unicorn cutter or stencil

METHOD

1. Preheat the oven as above.

2. Beat the butter and the sugar together until smooth.

3. Stir in the flour to get a smooth paste. Turn on to a work surface and gently roll out until the paste is 1cm/½in thick.

4. Using your cutter or stencil cut out your unicorns and place onto a baking tray. Chill in the fridge for 20 minutes.

5. Bake in the oven for 15-20 minutes, or until pale golden-brown. Set aside to cool.

To decorate

Ask a grown up to carefully melt the white chocolate in the microwave or in a bowl over a pan of hot water.
Use the chocolate to decorate the horn, mane, add eyes and anything else you would like!
Then add your rainbow sprinkles or other decorations to decorate the mane. Eat and enjoy!

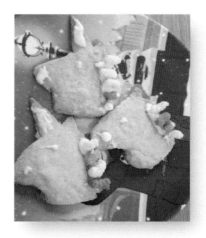

OTHER

TRUFFLES

Contributed by: Bayleaf Cookery School

Makes about 40 truffles

INGREDIENTS

200ml double cream
200g dark chocolate, chopped into chunks

METHOD

1. Pour the double cream into a saucepan and heat it over a medium heat until the cream is just about to boil—small bubbles will appear at the edge of the cream.

2. Remove it from the heat and leave for a few moments then tip the chocolate pieces in and stir gently until all of the chocolate has melted leaving you with a smooth, dark liquid.

3. Let the cream and chocolate liquid solidify (the quickest and easiest way of doing this is to put it in the fridge) until it's hard enough to scoop up with a spoon and roll it into balls - you choose the size. Roll each ball in cocoa powder (this stops them sticking to each other), then store them in the fridge.

4. There are loads of different flavour variations you can try - try adding orange zest, peppermint oil, cherry flavour, vanilla essence or anything else you fancy. You could also try using white or milk chocolate instead of dark, try rolling them in grated white chocolate or desiccated coconut instead of cocoa or maybe even try dipping the finished truffles in melted chocolate to give them a hard outer chocolate shell.

bayleaf
cookery school

@bayleafcookeryschool

Bayleafcookeryschool.co.uk

SLOW COOKER CHOCOLATE FUDGE

Contributed by: Jessica - Year 1

Cooking time: 1 hour

INGREDIENTS

500g milk chocolate (broken into pieces)
1 397g can condensed milk
15g butter

METHOD

1. Place all ingredients into the slow cooker.

2. Cook on low for one hour, stirring every 15 minutes.

3. While it is cooling, line a dish or baking tray with baking paper. We used a 7" x 11" tray that is 1.5" high.

4. Place the cooled mixture into the prepared dish or tray and put any topping on you want. We used white chocolate stars.

Alternatively you can make the fudge with 600g white chocolate instead of milk chocolate.
You can also mix different ingredients into the fudge.
You can even try caramel condensed milk.
There are so many flavours or combinations to try.

PLAYDOUGH

Contributed by: Erynn - Year 2

Makes one ball of coloured playdough

PLEASE NOTE THIS IS NOT FOR CONSUMPTION

INGREDIENTS

2 x mixing bowls
8 x tablespoons of plain flour
2 x tablespoons of table salt
60ml warm water
Food colouring
1 x tablespoon vegetable oil

METHOD

1. In one mixing bowl mix the flour and salt together.

2. In the second mixing bowl, mix the warm water, food colouring and vegetable oil.

3. Pour the bowl with water, oil and food colouring into the flour and salt mixture and mix well with a spoon.

4. Sprinkle some flour on a hard work surface. Empty the dough onto this work surface and knead together to make a smooth, pliable dough.

5. If you want a more intense colour add a few extra drops of food colouring and work into the dough.

6. Store in a food bag, air squeezed out, in the fridge.

Printed in Poland
by Amazon Fulfillment
Poland Sp. z o.o., Wrocław

64842659R00030